'Ukulele at School publi
www.Da

MW00574538

For audio examples, the latest news, and to contact us, please visit:
www.UkuleleAtSchool.com

Written by Steve Sano and Daniel Ho

Music performed and recorded by Daniel Ho

Consultants: Glen Kamida, Lydia Miyashiro-Ho,
Leonard Narumi, Gaby Thomasz, Linda Uyechi

Photo of Steve Sano and Daniel Ho (page 5),
and instructional images by Lydia Miyashiro-Ho

Photo of Steve Sano (page 38) by Linda Cicero, Stanford News Service

Jumping flea illustration by Doug Katsumoto

'Ukuleles in cover photo (left to right):

Baby Naturel 'Ukulele by Yoshihiro Naoki
http://homepage2.nifty.com/naokky/

Tiny Tenor 'Ukulele
Designed by Pepe Romero and Daniel Ho
www.RomeroCreations.com

Custom KoAloha Tenor
Polani (Pure), the first solo 'ukulele CD to receive a
GRAMMY nomination, was recorded on this instrument.
www.KoAloha.com

Cover artwork from Daniel Ho's GRAMMY-nominated CD,
On A Gentle Island Breeze, courtesy of Wind Music
www.WindMusic.com.tw

ISBN: 0-9833536-4-6
UPC: 644718011721

EAN: 978-0-9833536-4-5
Catalog number: DHC 80117

Table of Contents

Aloha Students

Welcome to the next step of your adventure in learning to play the 'ukulele! This is a follow-up to our earlier book, *'Ukulele at School, Book 1* (***www.UkuleleAtSchool.com***). In this second book, you will learn to play melodies as well as some of the basics of reading music. Because this book is based upon ideas you learned earlier, we recommend reviewing material from the previous book. Remind yourself of basics: how to hold the 'ukulele, how to use your left hand, and how to strum rhythms. It is important to have a solid foundation upon which to build the new skills you will learn in this book. We will also return to many of the songs you learned in the first book—not only will you learn new ways to play them, you and your classmates will be able to play both the new and old versions together as duets.

Remember to listen carefully to your teacher, and don't be afraid to ask questions if you need something explained again. We hope you enjoy learning even more about this wonderful, little instrument!

Aloha,   Mahalo,

Unit 1, Chapter 1
Tuning

Since you are already familiar with the basics of playing the 'ukulele, we want to introduce you to a slightly more advanced detail in tuning the instrument. To learn the ideas in this book, your 'ukulele will need what is called a **low G string**. That is, the fourth string (the string closest to your nose), should be tuned below the third string. Your teacher can show you how this works. Since not all 'ukuleles come strung this way, you might need to change the string on your instrument to the appropriate kind.

track 1

Your teacher will help you tune your 'ukulele. Listen carefully to the pitch of the string your teacher plays, then turn the correct tuner on your 'ukulele until the pitch matches your teacher's. If you are playing your 'ukulele at home, you can tune it to the audio example *track 1* at ***www.UkuleleAtSchool.com***.

Plucking

In the previous book, you learned how to strum. In this book, you'll learn to pluck individual strings. The easiest way to start doing this is to use your right-hand thumb. Use a downward motion and play on either your thumbnail or the flesh of your thumb.

Unit 1, Chapter 2 (Notes on the 1st String)
Playing the Note A

In the previous book, you learned how to play chords. Now, you'll learn how to play individual notes that can be put together to make melodies. For each note we introduce, we'll show you a photograph of how to play the note, a diagram of how to play the note, and actual written music of the note. The first note we'll learn is A.

The note A is very simple: just pluck the 1st string without touching it with your left hand.

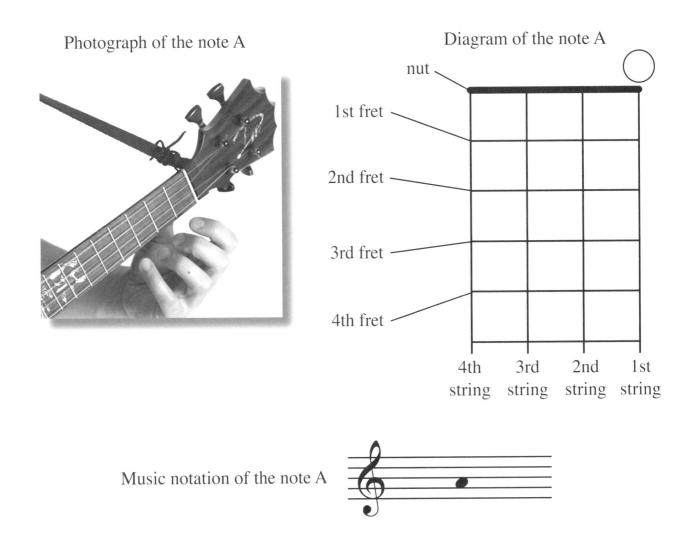

Photograph of the note A

Diagram of the note A

nut

1st fret

2nd fret

3rd fret

4th fret

4th string   3rd string   2nd string   1st string

Music notation of the note A

Above is an example of the note A as it appears in music notation. If you've never read music before, it's actually quite simple! Music notation is like using a picture to represent sounds. The five horizontal lines, and the spaces between them, represent specific notes, and the lines and spaces together are called a **staff**. At the far left of the staff is a symbol that is called a **treble clef**. The treble clef tells us how we are to read the notes on the staff; in this case, the second space from the bottom of the staff is an A. As we introduce additional notes, you'll see how different notes are represented by their placement at different positions on the staff. As you learn the different notes on the staff, it will be helpful if you memorize which notes appear on which line or space.

Here is a simple exercise to play the note A in rhythm. The note on the staff is the A that you just learned. One new thing to notice are the numbers $\frac{4}{4}$ (pronounced "four-four-time") to the right of the treble clef. We call this a **time signature**. It tells us how many beats are in each measure, and what kind of note gets one beat. In this case, the 4 on the top tells us there are four beats in each measure, and the 4 on the bottom tells us a quarter note gets one beat (so, a half note gets two beats and a whole note gets four beats—you'll only play half notes and whole notes in this exercise). You can refer to pages 11, 12, and 13 in *'Ukulele at School, Book 1* to review quarter note, half note, and whole note rhythms. Your teacher can review this with you in more detail. Remember to pluck each note with a downward stroke with your right thumb.

track 2

Playing the Note B

Here is the note B. On the staff at the bottom of the page, B is on the third line from the bottom of the staff (memorize this!). Use your left middle finger to play the 1st string at the 2nd fret.

Photograph of the note B

Diagram of the note B

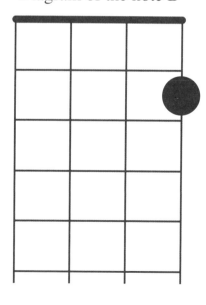

Music notation of the note B
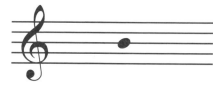

Here is an exercise to play the notes A and B in rhythm:

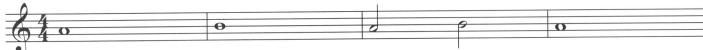

Playing the Note C

Here is the note C. In music notation, C is located on the third space from the bottom of the staff (again, memorize this!). Use your left ring finger to play the 1st string at the 3rd fret.

Photograph of the note C

Diagram of the note C

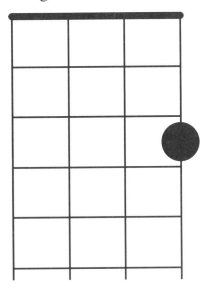

Music notation of the note C

Here is an exercise to play all three notes you've learned so far: A, B, and C. Note that this exercise is in a minor key. Just as with chords in a minor key, as you learned on page 22 in *'Ukulele at School, Book 1*', melodies in a minor key can sound sad or dark.

track 4

Now let's play an example using quarter notes in addition to the whole notes and half notes you've just played. Remember that a quarter note gets one beat, a half note gets two beats, and a whole note gets four beats. You can always go back to page 13 in *'Ukulele at School, Book 1*' to review quarter note rhythms. Also, notice that this exercise doesn't begin on the open (unfretted) A string; the first note in the exercise is a B!

track 5

Unit 2, Chapter 3 (Notes on the 2nd String)
Playing the Note E

The note E is very simple: just pluck the 2nd string without touching it with your left hand. Be careful not to pluck the strings next to the 2nd string.

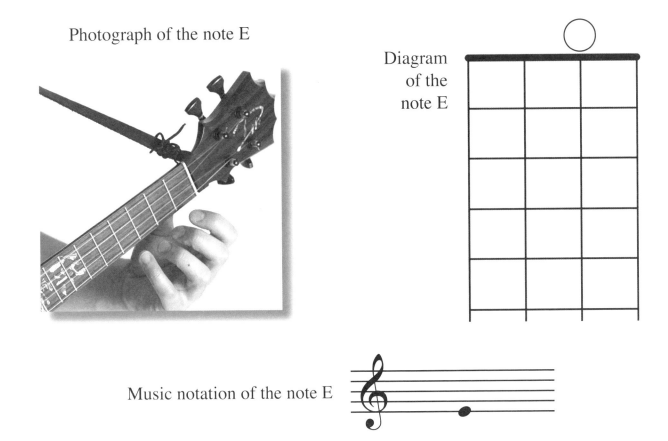

Photograph of the note E

Diagram of the note E

Music notation of the note E

Here's an exercise to practice the note E. We also re-introduce eighth notes in this exercise (you've seen eighth notes before, on page 14 of 'Ukulele at School, Book 1'). Look at the rhythm in the second measure: the first four notes are eighth notes and each one gets one-half beat, so they last only half as long as a quarter note. It is just like fractions in math! In this book, the eighth note is the shortest note you will play. Remember to always play an exercise slowly at first. Then, after you become comfortable with the new challenges, you can gradually speed up the tempo. We always like to say "if you can't play it slow, you can't play it fast!"

track 6

Playing the Note F

Here is the note F. Use your left index finger to play the 2nd string at the 1st fret. Remember, you should be memorizing how to read these notes on the staff as we introduce them to you.

Photograph of the note F

Diagram of the note F

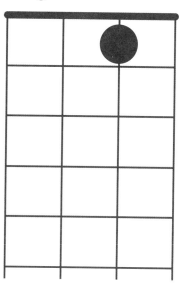

Music notation of the note F

Here's an exercise to practice changing from the note E to the note F. Notice that the rhythm is the same as the previous exercise, so if you're comfortable with the last rhythm, you can just concentrate on the changes between the notes E and F.

track 7

Playing the Note G

Here is the note G. Use your left ring finger to play the 2nd string at the 3rd fret.

Photograph of the note G

Diagram of the note G

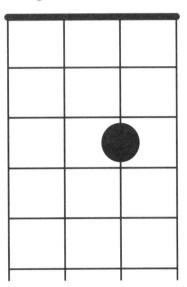

Music notation of the note G

And now here's an exercise to practice all three notes that you've learned on the 2nd string: E, F, and G. Remember that when you play fretted notes with your left hand, keep your fingers curved and play on the tips of the fingers.

track 8

Unit 2, Chapter 4
Crossing Strings

Now that you've learned to play notes on two strings, here's an exercise to practice playing notes on both strings. Think carefully about which notes are played on which strings: A, B, and C are played on the 1st string, and E, F, and G are played on the 2nd string. You can see why it's a great help to memorize the notes on the staff! Notice that the E that you play every other note is an open (unfretted) 2nd string. As you practice this exercise, make sure that your tempo stays steady as you switch from playing notes on one string to the other.

track 9

Here's another exercise to practice notes on both 1st and 2nd strings. But, unlike the example above, the repeating note in this exercise, which is an A, is an open (unfretted) 1st string.

track 10

Unit 3, Chapter 5 (Notes on the 3rd String)
Playing the Note C

You've already learned to play the note C on the 1st string, but now you'll play a different C on the 3rd string. You can actually play notes with the same names at several places on the 'ukulele. For this C, just pluck the 3rd string without touching it with your left hand. Be careful not to pluck the strings next to the 3rd string!

Photograph of the note C

Diagram of the note C

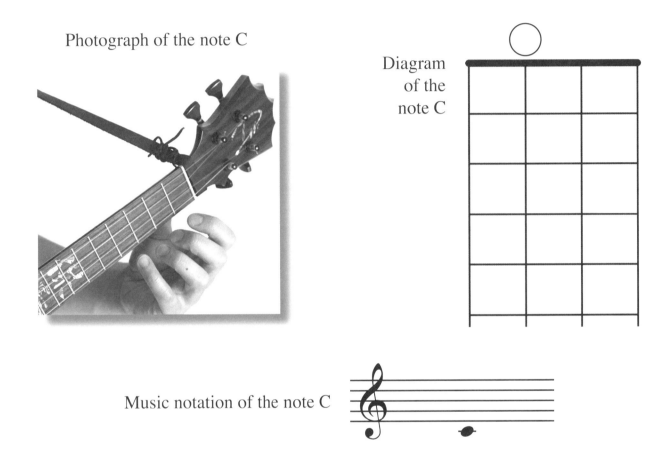

Music notation of the note C

Here is an exercise to practice the note C. Since you're so good at playing notes on open (unfretted) strings, we're going to introduce a new concept at the same time! With this example, we also introduce the concept of **dotted rhythms**. Look carefully at measure 2: notice that the first note of the measure has a small dot to the right of the notehead. The dot lengthens the note by half its original value. In this case, the notehead, a half note, tells you the note receives two beats—but the added dot makes it a total of three beats. We call this a **dotted half note**.

track 11

Playing the Note D

Here is the note D. Use your left middle finger to play the 3rd string at the 2nd fret.

Photograph of the note D

Diagram of the note D

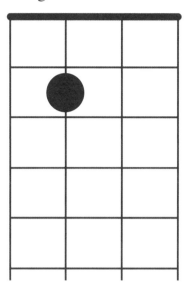

Music notation of the note D

Here's an exercise to practice playing the notes C and D on the third string. Notice that the rhythm for this exercise is the same as the previous exercise on page 16. This will give you more practice in playing dotted rhythms.

track 12

Unit 3, Chapter 6
Michael Row the Boat Ashore

Now that you've learned notes on the 1st, 2nd, and 3rd strings, you know enough to start playing song melodies. Most of these melodies are the tunes to the songs in *'Ukulele at School, Book 1*, for which you've already learned the strumming accompaniments.

Michael Row the Boat Ashore is an African American spiritual that you learned on page 25 of *'Ukulele at School, Book 1*. Here is the music for the melody. Notice that you don't play anything for the first three measures. The symbols you see in those measures (‑) are **whole rests**: don't play for four beats. The symbol you see at the beginning of measure 4 (‑) is a **half rest**: don't play for two beats. There are rests here because when we put the melody together with the strumming you learned for this song in *'Ukulele at School, Book 1*, you will need to wait for the introduction before playing the melody.

Remember that there are **repeat signs** in the first and last measures of music. This tells you to play the entire song over again.

Now that we're learning complete songs, it's a good idea to first learn and practice shorter sections of the song, then put the sections together after you're comfortable with each of them. For example, you can learn just measures 5-8 first. After you're comfortable with those measures, you can learn measures 9-12. Then, put the whole song together.

Here's the strumming accompaniment for *Michael Row the Boat Ashore* from *'Ukulele at School, Book 1*. After reviewing this, the music from the previous page can be played simultaneously with the music on this page—the two pages of music are meant to go together. Pair up with someone in your class to play and sing these two pages as a duet!

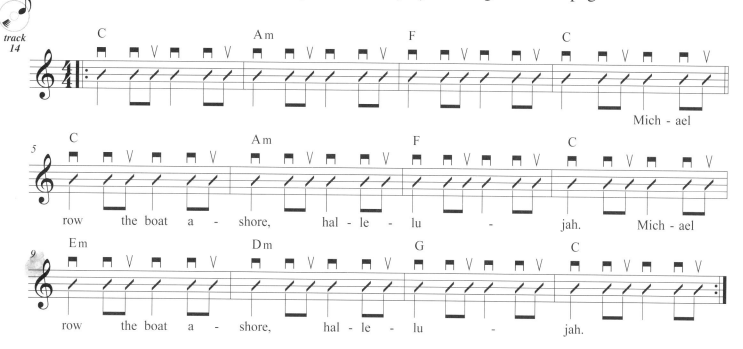

Sister help to trim the sail, hallelujah
Sister help to trim the sail, hallelujah

River Jordan is chilly and cold, hallelujah
Chills the body but not the soul, hallelujah

Jordan River is deep and wide, hallelujah
I've got a home on the other side, hallelujah

Then you'll hear the trumpet sound, hallelujah
Trumpet sound the world around, hallelujah

Trumpet sound the jubilee, hallelujah
Trumpet sound for you and me, hallelujah

Michael row the boat ashore, hallelujah
Michael row the boat ashore, hallelujah

Unit 4, Chapter 7 (Notes on the 4th String)
Playing the Note G

You've already learned to play the note G on the 2nd string, but now you'll play a different G on the 4th string. Just pluck the 4th string without touching it with your left hand. Very simple!

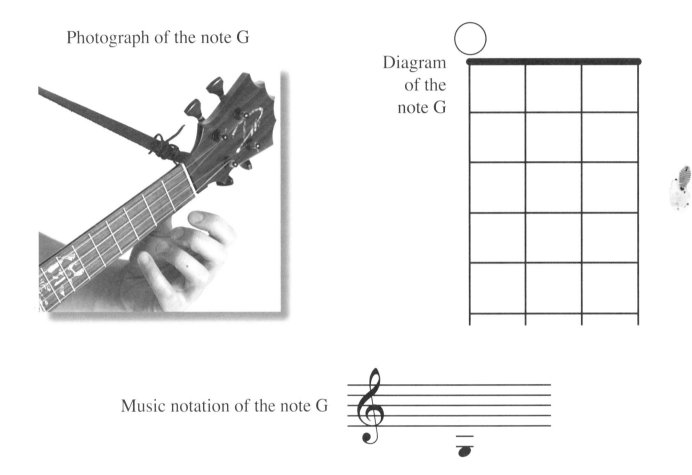

Photograph of the note G

Diagram of the note G

Music notation of the note G

Now let's do an exercise to practice playing the note G. With this exercise we introduce another dotted rhythm. Notice that in measure 2 the first note is a quarter note followed by a dot to the right of the notehead. As before, the dot lengthens the note by half its original value. So, instead of being one beat long, it's now one-and-a-half beats long. We call this a **dotted quarter note**. This dotted quarter note is followed by an eighth note (designated by a flag connected to its stem) that is half a beat long.

track
15

Playing the Note A

You've already learned to play the note A on the 1st string, but now you'll play a different A on the 4th string.

Use your left middle finger to play the 4th string at the 2nd fret.

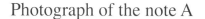
Photograph of the note A

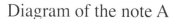
Diagram of the note A

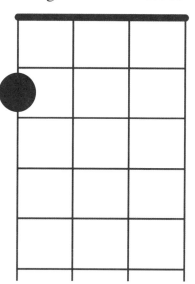

Music notation of the note A
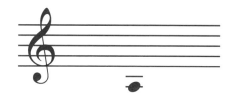

And of course, we need to play an exercise with both G and A on the 4th string! Again, we'll use the same rhythm that you played in the last exercise so you can concentrate on practicing the note changes from G to A.

Playing the Note B

You've already learned to play the note B on the 1st string, but now you'll play a different B on the 4th string. Use your left little finger to play the 4th string at the 4th fret. Be sure to memorize how the notes appear on the staff as you learn them.

Photograph of the note B

Diagram of the note B

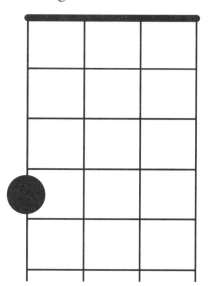

Music notation of the note B

Here's an easy exercise using the three notes you've learned on the 4th string, plus two notes on the 3rd string.

track 17

Unit 4, Chapter 8
Simple Gifts

Let's play another complete song. *Simple Gifts* is a song from the Shaker community that was composed in 1848 by Joseph Brackett. In this song you will use notes played on the 2nd, 3rd, and 4th strings. Remember to practice the song in shorter sections, and to practice slowly. When you become comfortable with all the notes and rhythms, you can gently speed up the tempo, but always play the song as smoothly as possible.

We've also written in chords above the melody. These are all chords you learned in *'Ukulele at School, Book 1*. Two people can play this together as a duet: one playing the chords, and the other playing the melody.

Unit 5, Chapter 9
Playing the Note B♭

We now introduce you to the note B♭. Use your left index finger to play the 1st string at the 1st fret.

Photograph of the note B♭

Diagram of the note B♭

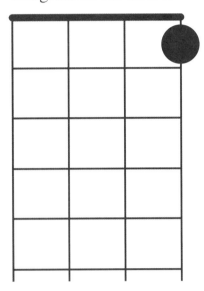

Music notation of the note B♭

Unit 5, Chapter 10
Clementine

Using the B♭ you just learned, you can play the complete melody to the American folk song *Clementine*. You learned how to strum this song on page 17 of *'Ukulele at School, Book 1*. Remember, we played the song with a swing-strum. To play the melody in the same style, wherever you see pairs of eighth notes, make them swing: the first note of the pair should be twice as long as the following note.

Note that the song is in ¾ time (pronounced "three-four-time"): there are three beats to a measure, and a quarter note gets one beat. Although the rest in the first measure is a whole rest as you've seen before, in this case it only gets three beats instead of four because the time signature of the song is ¾. The half rest in the second measure still gets two beats. Lastly, there's a repeat sign that tells you to repeat the music five times (to accommodate all the verses and choruses), and at the end of the song you skip to the final measure, marked with a "6."

Below is the version of Clementine you learned in *'Ukulele at School, Book 1*. You can use this to strum and sing along to the melody above.

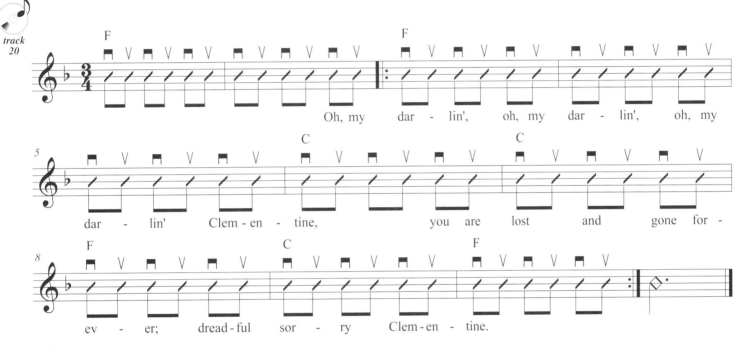

Oh, my dar - lin', oh, my dar - lin', oh, my dar - lin' Clem - en - tine, you are lost and gone for - ev - er; dread - ful sor - ry Clem - en - tine.

In a cavern in a canyon, excavating for a mine,
lived a miner forty-niner and his daughter Clementine.

> *chorus:* Oh, my darlin', oh my darlin', oh my darlin' Clementine,
> you are lost and gone forever; dreadful sorry, Clementine.

Light she was and like a fairy, and her shoes were number nine:
herring boxes without topses sandals were for Clementine. *(chorus)*

Drove she ducklings to the water every morning just at nine.
Stubbed her toe against a splinter; fell into the foaming brine. *(chorus)*

Unit 5, Chapter 11
Home on the Range

You should remember *Home on the Range* from '*Ukulele at School, Book 1*. It is a song from the American West and the state song of Kansas. It was composed by Daniel Kelley, with words by Brewster Higley. When you play the melody on this page, the rests at the beginning and the end are there so that it will fit with the version you learned before.

We suggest that when you start playing the melody, you have your left hand index finger already on the 2nd string at the 1st fret so that it's in place even before you pluck the first two notes on the 3rd string. Always look for ways to make your playing easier and smoother!

On this page is the version of *Home on the Range* from *'Ukulele at School, Book 1*. Remember to use the swing-strum when you play this. You can play this song as a duet with one person playing the music on this page, while another person plays the music on the previous page at the same time. When you play a duet, you should always listen carefully to the person playing the melody so that your strumming doesn't drown them out!

Unit 5, Chapter 12
Amazing Grace

Now we'll learn the melody to the familiar song *Amazing Grace*. The melody comes from the American folk tune *New Britain*. As you've seen before, there are rests at the beginning of the song so it will fit with the version from *'Ukulele at School, Book 1*. Because you used the swing-strum to play the version in the first book, you can swing all the pairs of eighth notes when you play the melody.

Here's the version of *Amazing Grace* from *'Ukulele at School, Book 1*. Remember to use the swing-strum to play this. In the previous song, we mentioned the importance of listening to other people playing the melody while you're strumming. Singing the song gives us another way to listen to the melody. As you strum this song from the music below, listen not just to the melody, but also to the words being sung. If you can't hear the words, you're playing too loudly!

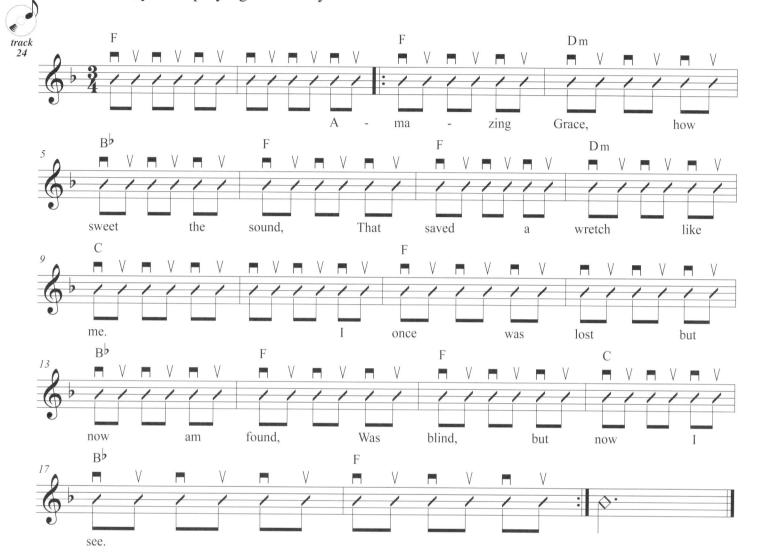

'Twas Grace that taught my heart to fear.
And Grace, my fears relieved.
How precious did that Grace appear
The hour I first believed.

Through many dangers, toils and snares
I have already come;
'Tis Grace that brought me safe thus far
and Grace will lead me home.

Unit 5, Chapter 13
Oh! Susanna

In order to play the melody to *Oh! Susanna*, you'll have to learn the note D played on the 1st string. Use your left little finger to play the 1st string at the 5th fret. This is the highest note you'll learn to play in this book.

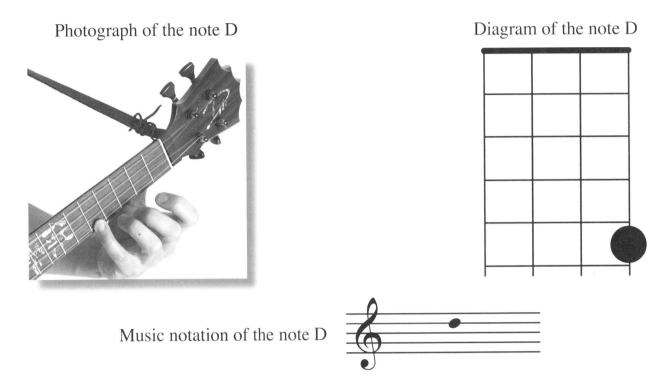

Photograph of the note D

Diagram of the note D

Music notation of the note D

The melody to Stephen Foster's song *Oh! Susanna* can be played on just the 1st and 2nd strings. This song is the first time you will play a note at the 5th fret. Because you must do this with the little finger, and the pinky is the weakest of all the fingers, practice reaching for the 5th fret with your little finger while your middle finger holds down the 1st string at the 3rd fret, as it will in measure 5. Also practice reaching for the 5th fret with your little finger while your index finger holds down the 1st string at the 1st fret, as it will in measure 13. This will help stretch how far you can reach with your fingers!

track 25

In this version of *Oh! Susanna* from *'Ukulele at School, Book 1*, we suggest using the accented horse-strum. This will provide an energetic accompaniment to the melody on the opposite page!

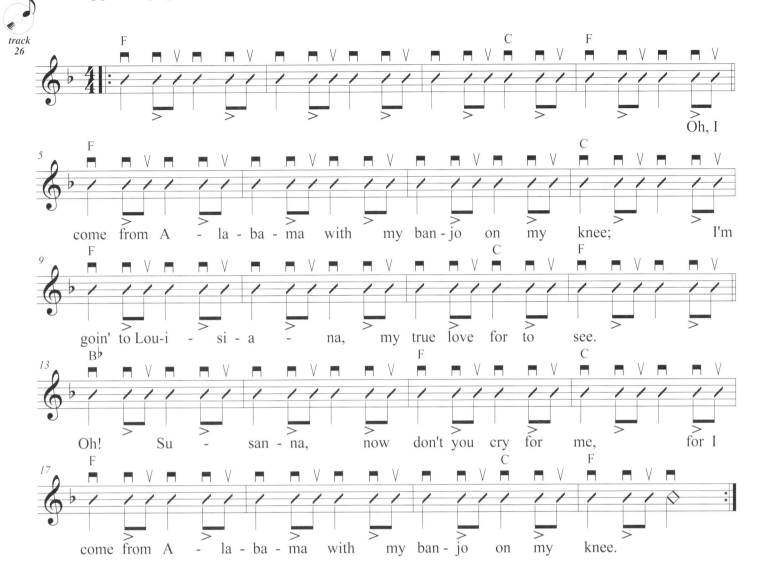

It rained all night the day I left; the weather was so dry.
The sun so hot I froze to death; Susanna, don't you cry.

    chorus: Oh! Susanna, now don't you cry for me,
                    for I come from Alabama with my banjo on my knee.

I had a dream the other night when everything was still;
I thought I saw Susanna, a-comin' down the hill. *(chorus)*

A buckwheat cake was in her mouth; a tear was in her eye.
I said, "I come from Dixie Land; Susanna, don't you cry!" *(chorus)*

Unit 5, Chapter 14
Playing the Note B♭

Before we move on to learning the next song, we introduce you to one more note. Here is the note B♭ on the 4th string. Use your left ring finger to play the 4th string at the 3rd fret.

You can hear that this B♭ is the same note as the B♭ you learned before on the 1st string, but sounds lower. If you play the two B♭s together, can you hear that one is higher and one is lower? These notes are what we call an **octave** apart. Your teacher can explain this in more detail, as well as review all the notes you've learned that are one octave apart.

Photograph of the note B♭

Diagram of the note B♭

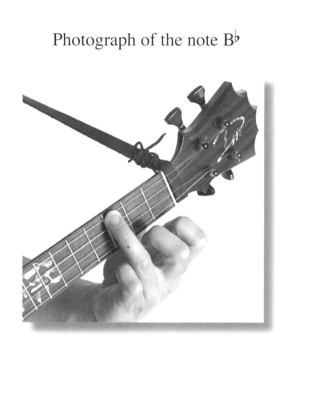

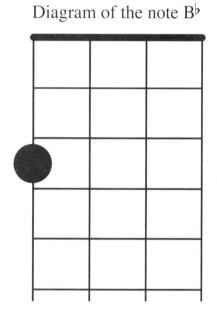

Music notation of the note B♭

Unit 5, Chapter 15
Diagram of Notes

Here is a diagram that conveniently shows all the notes you've learned in this book. You can use this as a handy reference when you need a reminder of how to play a specific note and don't want to flip through the entire book looking for the page where it was introduced. You might even want to bookmark this page so you can get to it quickly!

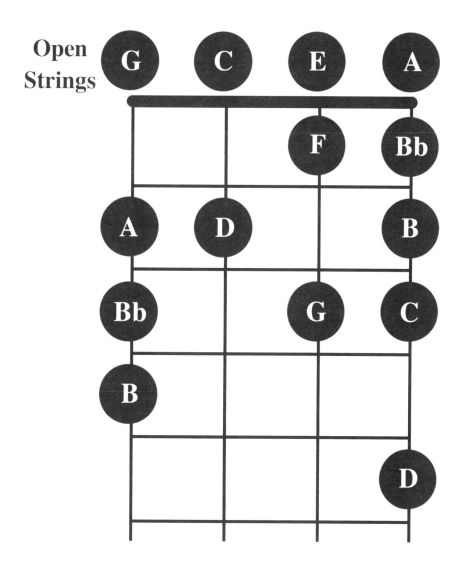

Unit 5, Chapter 16
The Ash Grove

Now we're ready to play the Welsh folk melody *The Ash Grove*. This wonderful melody has a larger range than any other in this book. This means that the distance between the lowest and highest notes of the song is the greatest of all the songs in this book. Also notice that you play both a B♭ and a B natural (meaning, it's not flat) in this song. Look at the third beat of measure 27 and you'll see a B with the symbol ♮ in front of it. This is a **natural sign** that turns it into a regular B instead of a B♭.

34

Here's the version of *The Ash Grove* from *'Ukulele at School, Book 1*. Review the "down, down-up-down" strum that you learned the first time you played this song, and keep the strumming smooth to fit the lyrical nature of the song.

Unit 5, Chapter 17

When the Saints Go Marching In

Now we'll return to the American gospel song *When the Saints Go Marching In*. This melody is played on just the two middle strings. Once again, there are rests at the beginning and end of the music to make it work with the strumming version on the next page.

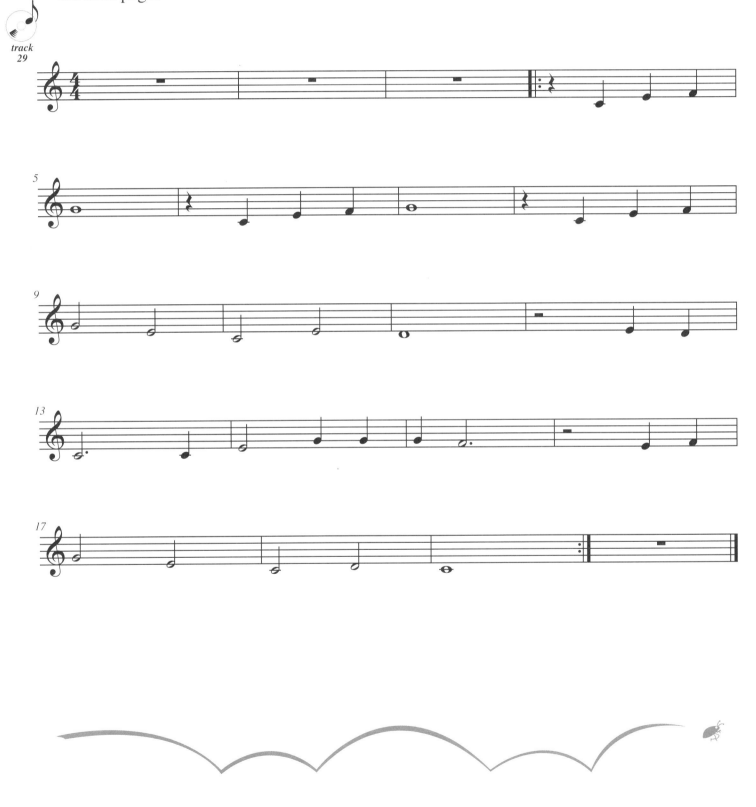

The music below should look familiar. As with previous songs, we're providing you with the version of the song you learned in *'Ukulele at School, Book 1*. Even though this music to *When the Saints Go Marching In* shows a half note strum, you can try playing this with the accented horse-strum that you learned at the bottom of page 26 in *'Ukulele at School, Book 1*—it'll have great energy that way!

track
30

Oh, when the band begins to play,
Oh, when the band begins to play,
Oh I want to be in that number,
When the band begins to play.

Oh, when the sun begins to shine,
Oh, when the sun begins to shine,
Oh I want to be in that number,
When the sun begins to shine.

Chord Chart

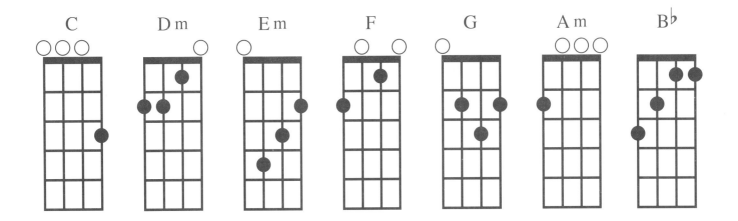

C   Dm   Em   F   G   Am   B♭

Ho'omaika'i 'Ana!

Ho'omaika'i 'Ana means congratulations in *Ōlelo Hawai'i*, the Hawaiian language! Congratulations on completing a full school year of learning the 'ukulele! Think about what you've learned over the course of these two books: you've learned seven chords that provide a great foundation for playing literally hundreds of songs. You've learned individual notes that let you play melodies to hundreds of songs. You've learned six different strumming patterns, some with variations. You've learned twelve songs that you can perform for, or even better, perform *with* friends and family. And most importantly, we hope you've learned how much joy it can be to make music.

The 'ukulele is like a great friend—it's best when you play with it! We feel that although it's "little," the 'ukulele is one of the grandest of all instruments because it's so easy to learn and you can always have it with you. It's definitely an instrument that's more fun to play than to listen to. We hope that learning to play is just the start of your adventure in making music with this wonderful instrument. *Ho'omaika'i 'Ana* again, and we wish you all the best on your future musical journeys!

Steve Sano

Daniel Ho